Using Fire

Focus: Systems

PETER SLOAN &
SHERYL SLOAN

A fire is hot. A fire gives heat. The heat from a fire can do many things.

A house can have a fireplace. The heat from a fire in the fireplace can keep us warm.

A gas oven uses fire
to make it hot. The heat
in an oven can cook
our food.

A gas kiln uses fire
to make it very hot.
The heat in a kiln bakes
pottery to make it strong
and hard.

A furnace uses fire to make it very hot.
The heat in this furnace can melt iron ore to make iron.

A steam train uses fire
to boil water. The heat
in a boiler turns water
into steam. The steam
makes the steam engine
run.

The sun is a huge fireball
far out in space.
The heat from the sun
makes all things grow
and keeps us warm.

Stage 1
1. Machines in the Home
2. Making a Car
3. Tools at Home
4. Floating
5. The Class Newspaper
6. From Grass to Milk
7. My Boat
8. Growing Beans

Stage 2
1. Using Machines
2. Electricity at Work
3. Parts of a Bike
4. Signs Everywhere
5. Sharing Time
6. Garbage Day
7. Baking a Cake
8. Front Loader

Stage 3
1. Flying Machines
2. Rain
3. Trains
4. Using Fire
5. Wheels at Work
6. Big Machines
7. Making Lemonade
8. Fences and Walls

Stage 4
1. Computers
2. Gasoline for the Car
3. Electric Motors
4. Making a Plane
5. Ships and Boats
6. Old and New Trains
7. Making a Tape
8. What If...?

Stage 5
1. Water for You
2. Making Electricity
3. Making an Ooze Monster
4. Machines in the School
5. Build It Big
6. Instruments
7. The Hospital
8. Machines on the Farm

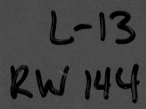

L-13
RW 144

K

Little Blue Readers—the next generation in the *Sundance family of books for emergent readers.*

Little Blue Readers begin at the emergent level for children ready for nonfiction. These books feature stunning photography with engaging, informational text. In fact, they are an early introduction to information reference books. **Little Blue Readers** are graded and keyed at every level to the following content strands:

Designing, Making and Appraising
Information
Materials
Systems

Teachers will find wide application for **Little Blue Readers** in the daily science and social studies work in their classroom. Children will enjoy the success of being able to read real "big kids" information written at their own reading level.

ISBN 0-7608-3171-8

9 780760 831717

S	T	A	G	E
1	2	3	4	5